WHO IS
ST. BASIL THE GREAT?

Micheline Nicoula

THE PARTHENOS PRESS

Contents

Introduction

St. Ambrose of Milan begins his work on Joseph the Righteous teaching us, "The lives of the saints are for the rest of men a pattern of how to live." Likewise, St. Paul the Apostle urges us in the New Testament, "Therefore, we also, since we are surrounded by so great a cloud of witnesses, let us lay aside every weight, and the sin which so easily ensnares us, and let us run with endurance the race that is set before us, looking unto Jesus."[1] Therefore, the lives of the saints from the Old Testament, New Testament, Church history and until our present generation always urge us to look unto our Lord and Savior Jesus Christ and when we study their lives and teachings, they remind us, "Imitate me, just as I also imitate Christ,"[2] as St. Basil himself teaches "The definition of Christian is the imitation of Christ."

Amidst the illustrious early Church Fathers, St. Basil the Great shines brightly as one of only

---

1   Hebrews 12:1–2.
2   1 Corinthians 11:1.

eight Church Fathers mentioned in the absolution of the ministers every liturgy, and as one of only three whose Anaphora we pray. It is a joy to introduce to you this book in your hands offering a concise, yet informative, exploration of this wonderful saint's life from his early formative years, his turning to God and service, and exploring his very influential writings. Despite its small size, the beautiful selections of St. Basil's writings within are evidence of why the Church chose to call him "the Great."

We thank our faithful daughter Micheline for her labor in researching the life of St. Basil and compiling these encouraging excerpts for the benefit of us all. We hope and pray that the Lord use this work to encourage us to disciple ourselves to the early Church Fathers and to seek and enjoy the life with God as they did.

Through the intercessions of the Mother of God, St. Mary, the prayers of the beloved St. Basil the Great and all the holy saints of his family, and the prayers of our honored fathers H.H. Pope Tawadros II and H.E. Metropolitan Youssef, may this work be for the glory of God and the edification of His Church.

Basil,

By the grace of God,

Auxiliary Bishop in the Coptic Orthodox Diocese of the Southern United States

September 23, 2024 / Thoout 13, 1741

The commemoration of the miracle performed by St Basil the Great

1

Early Life and Family

The title "Great" is attributed only to one among the three Cappadocian Fathers: Basil. His notable contributions as a Christian doctrinal exponent, ecclesiastical statesman, organizer, and a reformer of liturgy and oriental monasticism justify this title. St. Basil the Great was born around AD 329 as part of a wealthy Christian family residing in the city of Caesarea, Cappadocia.[1] Born to St. Basil the Elder and St. Emmelia, he was one of ten children in a wealthy family renowned for their piety and faith.[2]

The Influence of His Parents

His mother, Emmelia, renowned as the mother

---

1   Basil *Prolegomena.* In *Nicene and Post-Nicene Fathers: Second Series* 8, P. Schaff, ed. (Peabody, MA: Hendrickson Publishers, 2012), xiii. (Henceforth cited as NPNF².).

2   Ibid.

of saints, bore righteous children, despite the persecution her family suffered for their faith. Her father was martyred.[3] His father, a successful rhetorician at Neocaesarea in Pontus, ensured that his children received a good education. St. Basil received his early education from his father and then attended the schools of rhetoric in his native Caesarea, at Constantinople, and finally, after AD 351, at Athens.[4]

Grandmother's Impact

His paternal grandmother, St. Macrina the Elder, was a significant influence on her grandchildren, including St. Basil and his siblings. St. Basil mentioned her in two of his letters, crediting her as the one who first taught him about God. St. Macrina the Elder converted to Christianity through the teachings of St. Gregory the Wonderworker, the Bishop of Neocasearea.[5] She learned many things from her spiritual father and elder.

In his letter to the Neocaesareans, he expressed how it was "the illustrious Macrina" who "guarded … and formed and moulded me, still a child, in doctrines of piety." He says:

What clearer evidence can there be of my

---

3   Ibid.

4   Ibid., xv.

5   Ibid.

faith, than that I was brought up by my grandmother, blessed woman, who came from you? I mean the celebrated Macrina who taught me the words of the blessed Gregory; which, as far as memory had preserved down to her day, she cherished herself, while she fashioned and formed me, while yet a child, upon the doctrines of piety.[6]

And in another letter, he says:

The teaching about God which I had received as a boy from my blessed mother and my grandmother Macrina, I have ever held with increased conviction. On my coming to ripe years of reason I did not shift my opinions from one to another, but carried out the principles delivered to me by my parents. Just as the seed when it grows is first tiny and then gets bigger but always preserves its identity, not changed in kind though gradually perfected in growth, so I reckon the same doctrine to have grown in my case through gradually advancing stages. What I hold now has not replaced what I held at the beginning.[7]

---

6   Basil *The Letters* 204.6 (NPNF² 8: 245).

7   Basil *The Letters* 223.3 (NPNF² 8: 263–264).

Persecution[8]

St. Macrina the Elder ran away with her family, and they lived for about 7 years basically running away from being persecuted, so that they would not die. The persecutions were atrocious during the time of Diocletian, so all they could do is to flee.

St. Basil the Elder, the father of St. Basil the Great, worked a lot—he was a lawyer and a rhetorician—to provide for his family.

So, he established the estates of his family. St. Basil himself and his family grew up fairly wealthy, he was living affluent and rich life, and they were well known in the area. They lost all their wealth, however, in the time of persecution but later were able to regain their properties.

Siblings and Their Influence

St. Basil had several notable siblings. His older sister, St. Macrina the Younger, had a profound impact on St. Basil's spiritual life. She vowed virginity at the age of 12,[9] and began living an ascetic life in her home. She lived a deep life with God. After her father departed she encouraged her

---

8   See *The Catholic Encyclopedia* 9, C.G. Herbermann, E.A. Pace, C.B. Pallen, T.J. Shahan, and J.J. Wynne, eds. (New York, NY: The Encyclopedia Press, INC, 1913), 508.

9   See Gregory of Nyssa, *Life of St. Macrina*, Lowther W.K., ed. (London, UK: Society for Promoting Christian Knowledge, 1916), 24–25.

mother Emmelia to convert their home in Pontus to a convent and welcomed all the women that vowed virginity, helping them to grow in their relationship with God. St. Macrina the Younger had an immense impact on St. Basil the Great; she was a pivotal reason for the turning point that changed him to become more of a godly man. He already had the foundation from his family but he was busy with his career and studies. But she encouraged him to leave behind the worldly pursuits and live a deeper relationship with God.[10]

St. Gregory of Nyssa wrote about her, saying that she pushed St. Basil to live a deeper life with God:

> Macrina's brother, the great Basil, returned after his long period of education, already a practiced rhetorician. He was puffed up beyond measure with the pride of oratory and looked down on the local dignitaries, excelling in his own estimation all the men of leading and position. Nevertheless Macrina took him in hand, and with such speed did she draw him also toward the mark of philosophy that he forsook the glories of this world and despised fame gained by speaking, and deserted it for this busy life where one toils with one's hands. His renunciation of property was complete, lest anything should

---

10 Ibid., 28.

impede the life of virtue.[11]

Two of his brothers, Sts. Gregory of Nyssa and Peter of Sebastes, became bishops. Another brother, St. Naucratius, passed away at age 20, a loss that deeply affected St. Basil and spurred his pursuit of a life with God.

Friendship with St. Gregory the Theologian

St. Basil was a close friend of St. Gregory the Theologian, and the two often are depicted together. St. Gregory describes their friendship in a funeral oration for his lifelong friend St. Basil, saying:

We were contained by Athens, like two branches of some river-stream, for after leaving the common fountain of our fatherland, we had been separated in our varying pursuit of culture, and were now again united by the impulsion of God no less than by our own agreement. I preceded him by a little, but he soon followed me, to be welcomed with great and brilliant hope.[12]

This was the prelude of our friendship. This was the kindling spark of our union: thus we felt the wound of mutual love. Then

11 Ibid., 27–28.

12 Gregory Nazianzen *Oration XLIII* 15 (NPNF² 7: 400).

something of this kind happened, for I think it right not to omit even this.[13]

And when, as time went on, we acknowledged our mutual affection, and that philosophy was our aim, we were all in all to one another, housemates, messmates, intimates, with one object in life, or an affection for each other ever growing warmer and stronger. Love for bodily attractions, since its objects are fleeting, is as fleeting as the flowers of spring. For the flame cannot survive, when the fuel is exhausted, and departs along with that which kindles it, nor does desire abide, when its incentive wastes away. But love which is godly and under restraint, since its object is stable, not only is more lasting, but, the fuller its vision of beauty grows, the more closely does it bind to itself and to one another the hearts of those whose love has one and the same object. This is the law of our superhuman love.[14]

Such were our feelings for each other, when we had thus supported, as Pindar has it, our "well-built chamber with pillars of gold," as we advanced under the united influences of

---

13 Gregory Nazianzen *Oration XLIII* 17 (NPNF[2] 7: 401).
14 Gregory Nazianzen Oration *XLIII* 19 (NPNF[2] 7: 401).

God's grace and our own affection. Oh! how can I mention these things without tears. We were impelled by equal hopes, in a pursuit especially obnoxious to envy, that of letters. Yet envy we knew not, and emulation was of service to us. We struggled, not each to gain the first place for himself, but to yield it to the other; for we made each other's reputation to be our own. We seemed to have one soul, inhabiting two bodies. And if we must not believe those whose doctrine is "All things are in all;" yet in our case it was worthy of belief, so did we live in and with each other. The sole business of both of us was virtue, and living for the hopes to come, having retired from this world, before our actual departure hence. With a view to this, were directed all our life and actions, under the guidance of the commandment, as we sharpened upon each other our weapons of virtue; and if this is not a great thing for me to say, being a rule and standard to each other, for the distinction between what was right and what was not. Our associates were not the most dissolute, but the most sober of our comrades; not the most pugnacious, but the most peaceable, whose intimacy was most profitable: knowing that it is more easy to be tainted with vice, than to impart virtue; just as we can more readily be infected with a disease, than bestow health. Our most cherished studies were not the most pleasant, but the most excellent; this being one means of forming young minds in a virtuous or vicious mould.[15]

Two ways were known to us, the first of greater value, the second of smaller consequence: the one leading to our sacred buildings and the teachers there, the other to secular instructors. All others we left to those who would pursue them—to feasts, theatres, meetings, banquets. For nothing is in my opinion of value, save that which leads to virtue and to the improvement of its devotees. Different men have different names, derived from their fathers, their families, their pursuits, their exploits: we had but one great business and name—to be and to be called Christians.[16]

---

15   Gregory Nazianzen *Oration XLIII* 20 (NPNF[2] 7: 402).
16   Gregory Nazianzen *Oration XLIII* 21 (NPNF[2] 7: 402).

2

Turning to God and Service

Transition to Ascetic Life

St. Basil was well-educated in law and was initially secular, but after spending his youth in rhetorical studies, St. Basil experienced a spiritual awakening.[17] He said:

> Much time had I spent in vanity, and had wasted nearly all my youth in the vain labor which I underwent in acquiring the wisdom made foolish by God. Then once upon a time, like a man roused from deep sleep, I turned my eyes to the marvelous light of the truth of the Gospel, and I perceived the uselessness of "the wisdom of the princes of this world, that come to naught." (1 Cor.

---

17   See Basil *Prolegomena* (NPNF² 8: xvi).

2:6). I wept many tears over my miserable life and I prayed that guidance might be vouchsafed me to admit me to the doctrines of true religion.[18]

He was baptized, and embarked on a journey through Egypt, Palestine, Syria, and Mesopotamia to meet the most famous ascetics of the time, and was deeply inspired by their lives.[19]

About this, St. Basil said:

> I admired their continence in living, and their endurance in toil; I was amazed at their persistency in prayer, and at their triumphing over sleep; subdued by no natural necessity, ever keeping their souls' purpose high and free, in hunger, in thirst, in cold, in nakedness, they never yielded to the body; they were never willing to waste attention on it; always, as though living in a flesh that was not theirs, they showed in very deed what it is to sojourn for a while in this life, and what to have one's citizenship and home in heaven. All this moved my admiration. I called these men's lives blessed, in that they did indeed show that they "bear about in their body the dying of Jesus." (2 Cor. 4:10). And I prayed that I, too, as far as

---

18 Basil *The Letters* 223.2 (NPNF² 8: 263).

19 See Basil *Prolegomena* (NPNF² 8: xvii).

in me lay, might imitate them.[20]

St. Basil was particularly influenced by the monastic life in Egypt, and later wrote Rules for the ascetic life.

Return to Ascetic Life and Teachings

After living an ascetic life in the monasteries, St. Basil returned to Pontus divided his fortune among the poor and established a monastery.[21] Basil was soon to share the cenobitic life with companions near Neocaesarea on the Iris.[22] During this period, he wrote several influential works which earned him the name of Lawgiver of Greek Monasticism, he wrote homilies on the first six days of creation, and often spoke of nature's beauty and the reminders it provides of the Creator's majesty. In year AD 358 he was visited by his lifetime friend St. Gregory of Nazianzus and together they compiled *The Philocalia*[23] as well as the two monastic rules.[24]

Basil's Episcopal Role and His Fight for Orthodoxy

---

20 Basil *The Letters* 223.2 (NPNF² 8: 263).

21 See Basil *Prolegomena* (NPNF² 8: xvi–xviii).

22 Ibid., xvii.

23 Ibid., xviii.

24 Ibid., lii.

Basil was ordained a priest around AD 364[25] and later succeeded Eusebius as the bishop of Caesarea in AD 370.[26] He established hospitals, homes for the poor, and hospices for travelers and strangers.[27] He is known as one of the first to institute hospitals, a concept he incorporated into his teachings on social justice. He believed that those who had more than they needed should give to those in need, and equated hoarding with theft. He also fought ceaselessly against state-supported Arianism and stood firm against Emperor Valens and his prefects.[28]

Basil's Efforts for Unity

Basil's primary concern was the unity of the Church. He sought the patronage of St. Athanasius[29] in an attempt to establish better relations between Rome and the Orient, and even wrote to Pope Damasus[30] seeking a visit from him to the Churches in the East.

---

25 Ibid., xix.

26 Ibid., xxii.

27 See Gregory Nazianzen *Oration XLIII* 63 (NPNF[2] 7).

28 See Basil *Prolegomena* (NPNF[2] 8: xxiii–xxiv).

29 See Basil *The Letters* 66 (NPNF[2] 8: 163–164).

30 Basil *The Letters* 70 (NPNF[2] 8: 166–167).

3

The Writings of St. Basil

Basil was not just an ecclesiastical administrator and organizer, he was also a great theologian, and his writings were highly esteemed by contemporaries for their content and form. Basil's dogmatic writings were devoted to the overthrow of Arianism, and his ascetic writings included a number of works attributed to him, as well as some works whose authorship is disputed.

1. Dogmatic writings

Against Eunomius circa 363-365

Consisting of three books, book one, refutes the heresy of Arianism and refutes the idea that the Word cannot be the true Son of God. Book two defends the Nicene faith formula that the Word is con-substantial with the Father. Book three is about the con-substantiality of the Holy Spirit.

On the Holy Spirit

St. Basil composed this book in defense of the Divinity of the Holy Spirit.

2. Ascetic writings

A group of thirteen writings about monasticism.

3. Moralia

Overview

The Moralia represents Basil's first ascetic work, composed during his sojourn at the Iris in Pontus while Gregory of Nazianzus was with him. It is a collection of eighty rules or moral instructions, each supported by quotations from the New Testament.

Significance

The Moralia is notable as the oldest and most important piece of the *Corpus asceticum*. It primarily admonishes towards the ascetic life and is addressed to Christians.

4. The Two Monastic Rules

The Detailed Rules (*Regulae fusius tractatae*) and the Short Rules (*Regulae brevius tractatae*) are two sets of rules of later origin. They discuss the principles of monastic life and their application to the day-to-day life of a cloistered community.

5. Educational Treatises

Ad adolescentes

In his Exhortation to Youths, Basil discusses the value of Greek classical literature for educational purposes. He acknowledges the advantages of an education that combines Christian truth and classical culture.

Admonitio ad filium spiritualem

This Latin tract, of uncertain authorship, is likely influenced by early Egyptian monasticism.

6. Homilies and Sermons

In Hexaemeron

Basil's nine homilies on Hexaemeron, the narrative of the six days of creation, holds a place of honor among his homilies. They are notable for their rhetorical beauty and Basil's attempt to provide a

Christian idea of the world in contrast to the pagan one.

Homilies on the Psalms

Of the 17 homilies on the Psalms attributed to Basil, only 13 are likely authentic.[31] They provide a moral application rather than an exegetical interpretation of the Psalms.

Commentary on Isaiah

Basil's lengthy Commentary on Isaias 1-16 borrows heavily from Eusebius' commentaries.[32] The authorship of this commentary is contested, but it is significant for its sermons or lectures delivered by Basil in Neocaesarea.

7. Letters

The letters of St. Basil reveal his fine education and literary prowess. They can be categorized as follows:

Letters of Friendship

Basil had a strong desire for friendship and loyalty. The letters exchanged with friends for sharing ideas, consolation, encouragement, and advice

---

31   See Basil *Prolegomena* (NPNF[2] 8: xliv).

32   Ibid., xlix.

are particularly numerous. He often expressed his eagerness to hear from his friends and frequently requested that they write in return.

Letters of Recommendation

Basil wrote numerous letters to high authorities and wealthy individuals to recommend the poor and oppressed, to intercede for cities and towns, and for relatives and friends. His correspondence with Libanius of Antioch, a renowned Greek sophist, is of particular interest. Despite the difference in their beliefs, the correspondence between these representatives of the Christian and Hellenistic worlds illustrates mutual respect and their being in good terms.

Letters of Consolation

These letters were expressions of sympathy addressed to those suffering a loss, living in depression, or being attacked by heretics.

Canonical Letters

These letters were written with the sole purpose of reestablishing order wherever disturbances had occurred or canon law had been neglected. They contain detailed ecclesiastical regulations regarding penitential discipline and are essential for its history.

Moral-Ascetical Letters

These letters were intended to promote morality and asceticism among the clergy, laymen, and religious.

Dogmatic Letters

These letters are important for the history of liturgy. For instance, Letter 207 gives an excellent description of the vigil service, and Letter 93 recommends daily Communion.

Historical Letters

With far-reaching contacts, Basil's letters represent a first-class source for the history of the Empire and conditions of State and Church, for the relations between East and West, and for the controversies between orthodoxy and heresy.

4

The Divine Liturgy According to St. Basil

Gregory of Nazianzus mentions Basil's reform of the liturgy of Caesarea.[33] The Liturgy of St. Basil, still employed in the Coptic Church and in the Churches of the Byzantine rite on certain days, is believed to be his work.

We ought to assume that the present Basilian Liturgy is somewhat different from the original one, in that certain sections (e.g. Intercessions) must have been added to it. Although it underwent many changes over time, the core remained and still gives evidence of being the work of a master of the Greek language. There is strong evidence to suggest that St. Basil composed or reformed an existing liturgy. This is supported by the consistent tradition of the

---

33   See Gregory Nazianzen *Oration XLIII* (NPNF[2] 7).

Byzantine Church and numerous testimonies found in ancient writings.

One account, attributed to St. Proclus, Patriarch of Constantinople, states that St. Basil noticed the weariness and indifference of the people during the lengthy liturgy.[34] To address this, he made efforts to shorten the liturgy and revive their enthusiasm. This testimony, found in a treatise on the tradition of the Divine liturgy, suggests that St. Basil's reform was motivated by a desire to combat the slothfulness of the people.

Further evidence of the existence of a liturgical text ascribed to St. Basil is found in a letter written by Peter the Deacon. In this letter, Peter, an Oriental monk, mentions a Liturgy of St. Basil that was known and used throughout the entire East. He even quotes a passage from it, highlighting its widespread familiarity and usage.[35]

---

34 See *The Catholic Encyclopedia* 2, C.G. Herbermann, E.A. Pace, C.B. Pallen, T.J. Shahan, and J.J. Wynne, eds. (New York, NY: Robert Appleton Company, 1907), 321.

35 Ibid.

5

The Theology of St. Basil

The teachings of St. Basil revolve around the defense of the Nicene doctrine against various Arian factions. His lifelong friendship with Athanasius was rooted in their shared cause. He adhered to the patriarch of Alexandria with unwavering devotion, recognizing him as the champion of orthodoxy. St. Basil asserts that nothing can be added to the Creed of Nicea, except perhaps the glorification of the Holy Spirit, and only because the topic was briefly mentioned by the Fathers of Nicea.

On the Eucharist, St. Basil's Letter 93 to Caesaria in AD 372 provides insight into the history of Holy Communion. It attests to the custom of daily communion, and the belief in the presence of the body and blood of the Lord.

6

Excerpts from St. Basil's Writing

On giving thanks

If we do not thank God for the good that he gives us in the present, we will be forced to appreciate its value when he takes it away from us. Just as the eye may sometimes fail to focus on what is too close, and needs a moderate distance, so too is the ungrateful soul deprived of past good in order to become conscious of its benefit.

Yet no one is without some reason to give thanks, if he has any sense. Life gives each of us many different experiences, and we might take the opportunity to contemplate deeper values and the worth of the goods we posses by comparing it with those whose measured allotment is worse than our own.[36]

On mourning

So then, one must weep with those who weep. When you see your brother grieve, repent over his sins, weep with him and take part. Thus you can correct yourself through the others' sorrows. For the one who sheds hot tears over his neighbor's sins cures himself while lamenting for his brother.[37]

On justice and mercy

It is therefore necessary for you to blend mercy and justice, possessing with justice and dispensing with mercy, according to what is written, "Preserve mercy and justice, and ever draw near to God." God loves mercy and justice; therefore, the one who practices mercy and justice draws near to God. It follows that every person should make a thorough self-examination. The rich should carefully consider their means, from which they intend to make offerings,

---

36 Basil the Great, *On Fasting and Feasts*, S.R. Holman and M. DelCogliano, trans. (Yonkers, NY: SVS Press, 2013), 116–117.
37 Ibid., 121.

in order to make certain that they have not wielded power over the poor, or used force against the weak, or committed extortion against those in a subordinate position. We are commanded to maintain justice and equity even toward slaves. Do not use force because you rule, nor commit extortion because you are able to do so, but show the qualities of justice even while the means of authority are available to you. It is no proof of reverence for God if you obey when you cannot do otherwise, but rather when you have the ability to transgress, and do not. If, after taking what belongs to the poor, you give back to the poor, you should know that it would have been better if you had neither extorted from them nor given to them.[38]

On humility

So then, tell me, why are you haughty as if the good things you possess come from yourself, instead of expressing gratitude to the Giver of these gifts? For what do you have that you did not receive? If then you have received it, why do you boast as if you did not receive it? (1 Cor 4:7). You have not come to know God through your righteousness, but God has

---

38   Basil the Great, *On Social Justice*, C.P. Schroeder, trans. (Crestwood, NY: SVS Press, 2009), 104.

come to know you through his kindness.... After grace comes judgment, and the judge will examine how you have used the gracious gifts you have received.[39]

Do not exalt yourself

Do you think you have accomplished something good? Give thanks to God lest you exalt yourself above your neighbor.... [An] example is the fall of the Israelites. When they exalted themselves above the nations whom they regarded as unclean, they in fact became unclean, but the nations were made clean: the righteousness of the Israelites became like the rag of a menstruating woman, but the wickedness and impiety of the nations was wiped away through faith.[40]

Lower yourselves

These passages, and the others like them, let us always recite to ourselves in order to combat our pride. Let us lower ourselves to exalt ourselves, imitating the Lord who descended from heaven into extreme humility and in turn was raised up from humility to

---

39   Basil the Great, *On Christian Doctrine and Practice*, M. DelCogliano, trans. (Yonkers, NY: SVS Press, 2012), 113–114.
40   Ibid., 115.

an appropriate exaltation. Indeed, we find that everything the Lord did is a lesson in humility.[41]

Again on humility

Strive after humility in such a way that you come to love it. Love it and it will glorify you. In this way you will travel the good road leading to glory.[42]

Be ready for the Lord's coming is at hand

Thus it is necessary and advantageous for all of us, brothers, to ready ourselves like travelers or runners, and once we have figured out how to make this journey as light as possible for our souls, to push on straight to the end of the path.[43]

Be attentive to yourself

Be attentive to yourself, and know that the rational part of the soul is also intelligent but the passionate part is also irrational. And the one exists by nature to rule, while the other exists to obey reason and be

---

41   Ibid., 116.
42   Ibid., 119.
43   Ibid., 166.

persuaded by it. So do not ever allow your mind, reduced to utter slavery, to become a slave of the passions; moreover, do not yield to the passions struggling against reason and let them transfer to themselves the rule of the soul.

The exact comprehension of yourself also provides entirely sufficient guidance toward the concept of God. For if you are attentive to yourself, you will not need to trace your understanding of the Fashioner from the structure of the universe, but in yourself, as if in a kind of small ordered world, you will see the great wisdom of the Creator.[44]

Know yourself

Where thoughts come to you that bring swelling and inflammation in the heart, let the memory of the creation enter into you, how you were created. "God took dust from the earth, and God molded the human being." When can you forget what is your own? You forget what is your own when you withdraw from the earth. If you never depart from the earth but remain connatural with the earth ... you have nearby the memory of

---

44 Basil the Great, *On the Human Condition*, N.V. Harrison, trans. (Crestwood, NY: SVS Press, 2005), 103.

your lowliness.[45]

The great Fashioner

For we are satisfied to know the sky rather than ourselves. Do not despise the wonder that is in you. For you are small in your own reckoning, but the Word will disclose that you are great. Because of this wise David, examining and seeing himself exactly, says, "Wonderful is your knowledge from me," I have discovered in wonder knowledge concerning you.

Why "from me"?

"Wonderful is your knowledge from me," and the craftsmanship that is in me, understanding by what wisdom my body is structured. From this small work of construction, I understand the great Fashioner.[46]

On the Psalms

The prophets, the historians, the law, give each a special kind of teaching, and the exhortation of the proverbs furnishes yet another. But the use and profit of all are

---

45 Ibid., 58–59.
46 Ibid., 32.

included in the book of Psalms. There is prediction of thing to come. There our memories are reminded of the past. There laws are laid down for the guidance of life. There are directions as to conduct. The book, in a word, is a treasury of sound teaching, and provides for every individual need. It heals the old hurts of souls, and brings about recovery where the wound is fresh.[47]

Praying the psalms

A psalm is soul's calm, herald of peace, hushing the swell and agitation on thoughts. It soothes the passions of the soul; it brings her license under law. A psalm is welder of friendship, atonement of adversaries, reconciliation of haters. Who can regard a man as his enemy, when they have lifted up one voice to God together? So Psalmody gives us the best of all boons, love. Psalmody has bethought her of concerted singing as a mighty bond of union, and links the people together in a symphony of one song. A psalm puts fiends to flight, and brings the aid of angels to our side; it is armor in the terrors of the night; in the toils of the day it is refreshment; to infants it is a protection

---

47   Basil *Prolegomena* (NPNF[2] 8: xlv).

to men in life's prime a pride, to elders a consolation, to women and adornment. It turns wastes into homes. It brings wisdom into marts and meetings. To beginners it is an alphabet, to all who are advancing an improvement, to the perfect a confirmation. It is the voice of the church. It gladdens feasts. It produces godly sorrow. It brings a tear even from a heart of stone. A psalm is angel's work, the heavenly conversation, the spiritual sacrifice.[48]

Different titles of Christ

For "through Him" comes every succor to our souls, and it is in accordance with each kind of care that an appropriate title has been devised. So when He presents to Himself the blameless soul, not having spot or wrinkle, like a pure maiden, He is called Bridegroom, but whenever He receives one in sore plight from the devil's evil strokes, healing it in the heavy infirmity of its sins, He is named Physician. And shall this His care for us degrade to meanness our thoughts of Him? Or, on the contrary, shall it smite us with amazement at once at the mighty power and love to man of the Savior, in that He both endured to suffer with us in our

---

48 Ibid., xlvi.

infirmities, and was able to come down to our weakness? For not heaven and earth and the great seas, not the creatures that live in the water and on dry land, not plants, and stars, and air, and seasons, not the vast variety in the order of the universe, so well sets forth the excellency of His might as that God, being incomprehensible, should have been able, impassibly, through flesh, to have come into close conflict with death, to the end that by His own suffering He might give us the boon of freedom from suffering.[49]

St. Basil to St. Gregory on the Holy Scriptures

The study of inspired Scripture is the chief way of finding our duty, for in it we find both instruction about conduct and the lives of blessed men, delivered in writing, as some breathing images of godly living, for the imitation of their good works. Hence, in whatever respect each one feels himself deficient, devoting himself to this imitation, he finds, as from some dispensary, the due medicine for his ailment. He who is enamored of chastity dwells upon the history of Joseph, and from him learns chaste actions, finding him not only

---

49   Basil *On the Spirit* 8.18 (NPNF[2] 8: 13).

possessed of self-command over pleasure, but virtuously-minded in habit. He is taught endurance by Job who, not only when the circumstances of life began to turn against him, and in one moment he was plunged from wealth into penury, and from being the father of fair children into childlessness, remained the same, keeping the disposition of his soul all through uncrushed, but was not even stirred to anger against the friends who came to comfort him, and trampled on him, and aggravated his troubles. Or should he be enquiring how to be at once meek and great-hearted, hearty against sin, meek towards men, he will find David noble in warlike exploits, meek and unruffled as regards revenge on enemies. Such, too, was Moses rising up with great heart upon sinners against God, but with meek soul bearing their evil-speaking against himself. Thus, generally, as painters, when they are painting from other pictures, constantly look at the model, and do their best to transfer its lineaments to their own work, so too must he who is desirous of rendering himself perfect in all branches of excellency, keep his eyes turned to the lives of the saints as though to living and moving statues, and make their virtue his own by imitation.[50]

---

50   Basil *The Letters* 2 (NPNF[2] 8: 111).

On fasting

Fasting is as old as humanity: it was legislated in paradise…. If Eve had fasted from the tree, we would not need this fasting now…. Now the manner of life in paradise is an image of fasting, not only insofar as man, sharing the life of the angels, achieved likeness to them by being content with little, but also because those who lived in paradise had still not dreamt up what humans later discovered through their inventiveness: there was still no drinking of wine, still no animal sacrifices, not to mention whatever else beclouds the human mind. It is because we did not fast that we were banished from paradise. So let us fast that we may return to it.[51]

On envy

Envy is pain caused by our neighbor's prosperity.

***

Envy is the most savage form of hatred. Favors render those who are hostile to us for any other reason more tractable, but kind treatment shown to an envious and spiteful

---

51 Basil the Great, *On Fasting and Feasts*, S.R. Holman and M. DelCogliano, trans. (Yonkers, NY: St Vladimir's Seminary Press, 2013), 57.

person only aggravates his dislike.... He is more distressed by the resources of his benefactor than he is thankful for the benefits received. Envious persons surpass every species of animal in brutality of behavior. Wild beasts do not possess a ferocity equal to theirs. When dogs are fed, they become gentle; lions become tractable when their wounds are dressed; but the envious are rendered more savage by kind offices.

***

As vultures are attracted to ill-smelling places and fly past meadow after meadow and pleasant, fragrant regions, as flies pass by healthy flesh and swarm eagerly to a wound, so the envious avert their gaze from the brightness in life and the loftiness of good actions and fix their attention upon rottenness.[52]

On solitude

Now solitude provides us with the greatest help towards this achievement, quieting our passions and giving leisure to our reason to uproot the passions completely from the soul. Just as animals if they are stroked,

---

52 Basil of Caesarea, *Saint Basil: Ascetical Works*, R.J. Deferrari, ed.; M.M. Wagner, trans. (Washington, DC: The Catholic University of America Press, 1962), 463–470.

are more easily subdued to desires, wrath, fears, griefs, the venomous evils of the soul, if they have been lulled to sleep by silence and have not been kept aflame by constant provocation, are more easily overcome by reason. Therefore, choose a place such as ours, removed from association with men, so that nothing from the outside will interrupt the constant practices of the ascetic life.[53]

On unceasing prayer

You will pray without ceasing, when you offer prayer that is not restricted to words, but also uniting it with God in all that you do in life. Indeed, your life should become an unceasing and uninterrupted prayer.[54]

On the life of piety and praise, and silent contemplation

Pious exercises nourish the soul with divine thoughts. What state can be more blessed than to imitate on earth the choruses of angels? to begin the day with prayer, and

---

53 Basil of Caesarea, *Letters (1–185)*, H. Dressler, ed., A. Clare Way, trans. (Washington, DC: The Catholic University of America Press, 1951), 6–7.

54 Basil the Great, *On Fasting and Feasts*, J. Behr, ed., S.R. Holman and M. DelCogliano, trans. (Yonkers, NY: St Vladimir's Seminary Press, 2013), 113.

honor our Maker with hymns and songs? As the day brightens, to betake ourselves, with prayer attending on it throughout, to our labors, and to sweeten our work with hymns, as if with salt? Soothing hymns compose the mind to a cheerful and calm state. Quiet, then, as I have said, is the first step in our sanctification; the tongue purified from the gossip of the world; the eyes unexcited by fair color or comely shape; the ear not relaxing the tone or mind by voluptuous songs, nor by that especial mischief, the talk of light men and jesters. Thus the mind, saved from dissipation from without, and not through the senses thrown upon the world, falls back upon itself, and thereby ascends to the contemplation of God. When that beauty shines about it, it even forgets its very nature.[55]

On prayers and union with God

Prayers, too, after reading, find the soul fresher, and more vigorously stirred by love towards God. And that prayer is good which imprints a clear idea of God in the soul; and the having God established in self by means of memory is God's indwelling. Thus we become God's temple, when the continuity

---

55 Basil *The Letters* 2.2 (NPNF[2] 8: 110–111).

of our recollection is not severed by earthly cares; when the mind is harassed by no sudden sensations; when the worshipper flees from all things and retreats to God, drawing away all the feelings that invite him to self-indulgence, and passes his time in the pursuits that lead to virtue.[56]

A defense of non-scriptural liturgical rites

Of the beliefs and practices whether generally accepted or publicly enjoined which are preserved in the Church some we possess derived from written teaching; others we have received delivered to us "in a mystery" by the tradition of the apostles; and both of these in relation to true religion have the same force. And these no one will gainsay;— no one, at all events, who is even moderately versed in the institutions of the Church. For were we to attempt to reject such customs as have no written authority, on the ground that the importance they possess is small, we should unintentionally injure the Gospel in its very vitals; or, rather, should make our public definition a mere phrase and nothing more. For instance, to take the first and most general example, who is thence who has taught us in writing to sign with the

---

56   Basil *The Letters* 2.4 (NPNF² 8: 110–111).

sign of the cross those who have trusted in the name of our Lord Jesus Christ? What writing has taught us to turn to the East at the prayer? Which of the saints has left us in writing the words of the invocation at the displaying of the bread of the Eucharist and the cup of blessing? For we are not, as is well known, content with what the apostle or the Gospel has recorded, but both in preface and conclusion we add other words as being of great importance to the validity of the ministry, and these we derive from unwritten teaching. Moreover we bless the water of baptism and the oil of the chrism, and besides this the catechumen who is being baptized. On what written authority do we do this? Is not our authority silent and mystical tradition? Nay, by what written word is the anointing of oil itself taught? And whence comes the custom of baptizing thrice? And as to the other customs of baptism from what Scripture do we derive the renunciation of Satan and his angels? Does not this come from that unpublished and secret teaching which our fathers guarded in a silence out of the reach of curious meddling and inquisitive investigation? Well had they learnt the lesson that the awful dignity of the mysteries is best preserved by silence. What the uninitiated are not even allowed to look at was hardly likely to be publicly paraded about in written documents.[57]

The blessings of communal prayers

A Psalm forms friendships, unites those separated, conciliates those at enmity. Who indeed, can still consider as an enemy him with whom he has uttered the same prayer to God? So that psalmody, bringing about choral singing, a bond, as it were, toward unity, and joining the people into a harmonious union of one choir, produces also the greatest of blessings, charity.[58]

On choosing a Spiritual Father

But with much care and forethought set about finding a man skilled in guiding those who are making their way toward God who will be an unerring director of your life. He should be adorned with virtues, bearing witness by his own works to his love for God, conversant with the Holy Scripture, recollected, free from avarice, a good, quiet man, tranquil, pleasing to God, a lover of the poor, mild, forgiving, laboring hard for

---

57   Basil *On the Spirit* 27.66 (NPNF[2] 8:40–42).

58   Saint Basil, *Exegetic Homilies*, A. Clare Way, trans. (Washington, DC: The Catholic University of America Press, 1963), 152.

the spiritual advancement of his clients, without vainglory or arrogance, impervious to flattery, not given to vacillation, and preferring God to all things else. If you should find such a one, surrender yourself to him, completely renouncing and casting aside your own will, that you may be found a clean vessel, preserving unto your praise and glory the good qualities deposited in you.[59]

✜ ✜ ✜

Conclusion

Basil passed away on January 1, AD 379, at the age of around 50 which according to the Julian calendar coincided with the 6th of Tobe, however after adopting the Gregorian calendar it now falls on the 14th of January and that is when the Coptic Church celebrates the Feast of his departure. However, the Eastern Orthodox churches celebrate on January 1st.

His life and works laid the foundations for unity and order in the Church, and he continues to be recognized for his significant contributions to Christianity. May the prayers of St. Basil the Great be with all of us.

---

59 Basil of Caesarea, *Saint Basil: Ascetical Works*, R.J. Deferrari, ed.; M.M. Wagner, trans. (Washington, DC: The Catholic University of America Press, 1962), 19.

7

Supplementary Material

The miracle performed by St. Basil the Great

On this day also is the commemoration of the great miracle performed by St. Basil, Bishop of Caesarea, Cappadocia.

A young man, who loved his master's daughter, was deceived by Satan, his enemy and the enemy of the human race. Satan made him resort to a magician who made him write a covenant to deny the faith and to surrender completely to Satan, so that Satan might grant him his wish. Satan kindled lust in the heart of the girl, and she loved the young man exceedingly. She asked her father insistently not to object to her marriage to that young man. Eager for his honor and fearing for her life, he gave her in marriage to him.

When she had spent with him a long period of

time, she noticed that he did not enter the church or partake of the Holy Mysteries, or make the sign of the holy Cross over himself. She revealed to him her doubt about his faith and his love of God. He told her what had happened to him, and how he had written to Satan a covenant of obedience till death.

She cried much and rebuked him for his deed. She took him to St. Basil, Bishop of Caesarea. He listened to the confession of the young man and saw his grief and desire to go back to the life of worship, fellowship, and righteousness. St. Basil comforted him and asked him to stay with him for a while in seclusion, fasting and praying. He shut him up in a nearby room for three days. On the third day St. Basil visited him and the young man told him that the evil spirits had not ceased disturbing and fighting him in many ways. He strengthened him, calmed him down, gave him food and prayed for him. St. Basil asked him to remain in seclusion, praying and fasting. After a few days, he came back to visit him again. The young man told St. Basil that he did not see the devils any more, but he still heard their cries and threats. St. Basil gave him food again and prayed for him and left him to the life of seclusion to fight and pray, and the bishop went to pray on his behalf also. And this went on until 40 days were completed. When the Saint came to him and asked him about his state, he told the Saint that he saw him [the Saint] fighting against Satan on his behalf, and he vanquished him and finally was victorious.

The Bishop gathered all the priests and the monks and prayed for the young man all that night. On the following morning he led him into the church while everyone was crying, "Lord have mercy on us," and they continued to cry out until that writing, which the young man had written as a covenant to deny the faith and to surrender to Satan, fell down in the midst of all the people. The Bishop, the young man and his wife, and all the people rejoiced exceedingly. The Bishop blessed that man and administered to him the Holy Mysteries. The man and his wife departed to their house full of joy for the peace and repentance they received. They praised God and thanked St. Basil by whose prayers they were saved.

The blessings of his prayers be with us all, and Glory be to our God forever.[60]

---

60   Coptic Synixarium, Paope 13